*Uninterrupted time*

International Poetry Studies Institute
Faculty of Arts and Design
University of Canberra
Canberra, Australia
http://ipsi.org.au

Poems © Alvin Pang 2019
Design: Caren Florance

ISBN 978-0-6485537-8-6

# Alvin Pang
## **Uninterrupted time**

IPSI CHAPBOOK 2.4

University of Canberra
International Poetry Studies Institute
Series editor: Paul Munden

When the world stops spinning will the plates fall off? Careful, you've reached the tip of the tongue. Better off without boats or guns, but look. Hokusai loved to draw maps of places he'd never been. First cranes, then the young wife who loves seafood. The taut string of a bridge he made up, the thirty-six views of an immovable object. Not even death could stop his laughter, his piss-pot missive to his prissy publisher. Art-mad old geezer, devotee of a star you cannot see from Australia. We sail blind knowing the tide must be. The line that shall not be stuck in the craw. The next logical leap, then back to tell of it. But how?

In this universe we sip milk tea as the child we can never have gambols on the fine sand of our unfinished pining. What we make in the vestigial night is not love but history. Every dawn we darn our verses by the filmy window while the kettle learns to whistle. This will bore you. You will want marks on paper to cut less cleanly. You want the breath to sizzle in the October air. I will reach for the granulated stevia and ask for a spoon. There is no spoon so I use the blunt end of a pen, something we would never allow our boy to do, had we, say, a boy and not indifferent carnations. We would have sorted out who was the good cop and who the bad before the third trimester, and not been at this loss of who to grieve and who to drive for groceries half-dazed from sleep. Or Netflix: always cooking shows with knife-work immaculate as habits, and perfect bakes. Every year, a new Disney tune to hum while trimming the wayward hedges. More dirt, more over there to patch the bare roots. Had we a garden.

Three lossy memoirs:

You asked me for a child. The sudden drop of another expectancy. The Empress will not forgive the loss of her prize peonies.

I begged for a stay of ten years. A niece|nephew waiting in utero, with unformed lungs, to come full term. Beginnings are also endings, drawled the Giver of Broken Wings.

The body most cruel when most itself. She can try again after for another. Who is made up to mask bad news.

I remember the song of your last kiss. Pray with you, the doc said, when asked what he could do. What is meant by what is meant to happen.

Mine among the least fertile countries in the world. Unviable but stubbornly there. Is the Goddess of Good Births a clinician or a sieve?

Where would we have lived, with our bundle of contradictions? Natural is kindest: let it snuff itself out without hard decisions. Who to turn to for unsafe passage?

We could have found a beach to walk, the three of us. There are people who make arrangements for this sort of thing (but they're not cheap). The Avatar of Goodbye selling fake watches on a pier.

Instead we trade floral jpegs and sunsets, avoid the unhatched questions. What name to give the newborn dead? If the Keeper of Secrets stole sips, who would know?

Buried: the chance to hold each other and weep. To mark a year hence with candles: a birthday, or...? Old Man Heaven shuts his eyes.

We practise failure in the car, my hand on the wheel and in your lap, your hand pressed to your cheek and draped over my bare thigh like a yellow dishcloth. The traffic practises failing to meet its flow quota. The rain fails to stop. The day manages to pass without a crack in the sky but the crack in the road takes several years off the suspension. I am not yelling at you, not really. Knowing it is there doesn't cushion the shock. Whenever, however it comes.

The man at the door, I've turned him away before. I've made my lover wait and not come. I've imagined silence and swallowed it, spat out static. I've thrown my brothers, tired of questions, out into the pale streets to seek God, start a band. I've put on martyrdom and buttoned up. I've been told my heart is in the right place (just behind and slight left). What sort it is the pain will not say, sharpens its knives for years till the glint shivers in moonlight and misstep, one laugh, one sabot across the cut grass. The measure between this hour and our departure, precisely the arch of uncusped wings over the dusk-loured hills. Too many in a humid room. Not even my child will thank me for her bones. I am no stranger to breaking.

My daughter begins to row. Distrusts old hillmaps produced by the Admiralty. Makes her own silence out of shoehorns and torn pages. Has adequate supplies. On one of her spacewalks she brings back an urn half-filled with my ashes. She prefers her own music for the dirge. She sorts through debris for gags to remember. All too soon the glass boat breaks. But she can swim and books I will never read line her shelves. An unmarked moon beckons with each sleep. Her farm on the edge of the balloon fruits secrets. She plans to live there among her pomegranates and leeches. The arc of her bones bends towards rain. She is readying wings for the sprint. One with the feathers of a crow. The other of a goat.

This being human, it's not my thing. A bowl of ramen can stand in for breath in Maruyama. The calm tiger, the snow leopard, the upsized glass of domestic draft, the accents we spent thousands to escape from, behind and before us in the cashier queue. Unused to sleet we meet the street face to face, claim insurance later. The winter, beautiful and thoughtless as children, darting about with no gloves on. A fist against the bare cliff of this escalation: adolescence. The king crab roasting on a common grill. Scallops tasting of a night away from love, the invoice paid on time, thus. What is it about the white that makes us want to dress it up in shape, knowing melt comes? No fortune slip ever says: forget the future and live if you dare. We clap our hands and ring the bell. We scratch to win. We breed in captivity.

A whole table of uninterrupted time: no alarms, chores, dinners, earthquakes, microwave disasters, spilt milk, unmarked essays, radio broadcasts, sirens, neighbourly complaints. Only the hush into which breath pours unto the ages unending, your uncreased boughs to east and west and pinioned and salted, salted well. Sudden attar, musk giving way to muskrose. Never the same nectar twice. Too blushed to ask for seconds. How tea tastes different sip to final sip.

What is this singing that we do? This keening in the blank dark. Nations thwarted by the dam, but so sweet the challenge: the tilted plough, an old image from before bottled lightning, the ether made glow. Those needlepoints behind the nimbus? Those uvular tides? Here are pebbles from the shore of our furlough. An outpost, not the palace fort. If we fall the sea will catch us. Mingled: a thousand years, the coin of our spent breaths. What we put in our mouths to still the wanting. What we free to keep serous, fluent.

The night you, handheld, limbsplayed, served up the sweet shallows to the salt of my lips as the bath bled heat, we were near the edge of empires, a gull's wingbreak from Atlantis. Uncrowned, you and I, returned to water, fleeing rain and the terror of flags. Always you wanted to be barely touched, lepidopterous, called on, not pinned. A thirst sipped risking hunger, wrinkled skin, discovery. Come dawn the ache of sleep gnaws like blind fish at the brink of our heed. Road before us, no names to leave behind for the chaste clouds to stumble over trying to call us back.

Words are waves, how the deep speaks from one shore to its other, and hunger too is a song of the road, its keening. He tells the raucous mynahs to carry his freight. The sun to send grass, from whose susurrations he learnt the language of caress. He remembers the pumafold of your back, the fleeting emberscar of your breath on his cheeks. Left on his lips, the promise of sea, the scent reached for on every coastline, you and him both, shy of storm, quickened at the prospect of rain, listening for bells with fingers on the mute, wet glass.

Where petals fall. Where crimson warms grey cobble. Where sunlight wets the dun contour, the inumbrated cleft. Where mead, swallowed, beads honey from the wrack. Where you bleed you sigh, make the sign for fire. Lost now, the brimming dugout, slipped home and well come. Vesselled, the cut bloom, dewed and held close. At the speed of tides. Chivved vespers: gasps. Litanies, limned from the throat to what waves. No shrine here but the worship, whorl-shaped, tacked to horizon, rock-steadied. How you lift me, drowning, unto the sudden shore.

Much upon the grass, brined by spray and the low brume of another scarp, me you locked and asked, tongue still spiced from the lash of malt, to bend. Something about how forms of a certain vintage crumb when touched, flint doffed and squammed, peppery, if grey in the glint. The scent between fingers of old moss, must musk, but parmesanal, fridged fust, estuarial on the sheets. Spent yeast. And you unrisen, all too summery then, insinuous, game but cautious of gain, unsodden and wary of ignition. Your eyes calid, the loom of you windward and parlous. I had to stop the wound from seeping, just in time.

Who wants to drown dry? Come now, brush against the burnished rock, bleed some light you still have. Loss limns access, not possession. None of that key yawn, unreeling from thwarted kiss to hot and tender moon. And then the bawl in the war zone, the turning away towards a bit more sleep. So seed was downed in the crack. So the ground gapes and lets the futile gametes reach a little into dawn, some months. Before water shunts the tap. But look what else stirs now, barren: the textskins, the songveils, the leather of spent hands, what shades swaddle with, trade breath for. All who have joy mislaid, sold their names to wind. To rustle. In the ears of the lost. To give birth to, from death, ado. Her nation of sough.

And yes I want the full sob of your red and yes the prickling of thumbs raised flagging what this way comes yes the quaking swing vote of the body politic yes referenda yes loose lips sunk deeper into the system ungovernable by wellplaced seaword salty cant become argot of gold if rare and shared enough between you and me yes i saw the eyewater you spent sparingly when time to brave the salacity of wings and disremember the crush of us the sweet teeming on the trim of where we lay gasping rescued our tongues freed of their homelands nubbed into newborn peculiarity as if the if were isthmus to where the yes which was still and still the yes which shall

He has counted your stars. He has placed a mouth on the borders of your silence. He has stepped through your shadows without flinching, without the need to draw maps. He has mended the cup and has sipped. Has swallowed and lived. Over these dunes, the heel trace of old caravans, the shudder of hooves through the long grass. Where there is water he has bent to, parched, grateful, called Beloved with mute lips, buried his tongue for another age to come. Where time has stained the torn silks, he reads a prayer for a song from a dream of unnavigable reaches. A river from which two bloods may draw their source. Part the curtains; step past the broken arches. Nothing is lost but waits to be made whole.

Afterwards, skin silvered in the late spring light, windows curtainless but kind, nigh hills roséd by dusk, you plashed across the dim doona like a swash of pearl, carnations agape on the sill, with only the velutinous tulle of now, milk spume not yet moietied into time, while love lives, spent into being, made current and moss-sown, deliquescent, still, because a room left quietly to itself intimates forever, because here we might yet have just been dancing in the old sweet way, with nothing to tell of what is out of frame, what travels and travels past the reach of light, what we hoped to hasp, where we thought to stop.

How to excise an act of love? The caress of one tongue against the grot of another's language? Might as well take the verb out of the sun's giving; the bed's mute bearing of flight. Not flight, not exactly, but a falling into. The declension of roots towards remembered dark; caliginous. The equality of push with pull, the tilt and elision of again, of the friction that is erasure. There is a word that means prayer through the body, and in speaking it what is made whole is forgotten. The white of it: debts dismembered as a clean kill is, sustains the raptor's chick. Back to knives then. The point being to open things. As seed does soil. As lips sunder refusal. The graft and gift this is.

Maybe it's because you feel segmented. Cut up. Earthworm in rich humus, burning at both ends. The cake does not cohere. Is that a donut or a bagel and must we choose between whorls? When is a not knot? Pottery or Proles? Ten ways to jumpstare your loaf life. Ah kong ah ma fighting pots and pans in the monsoon—a folk figure for uncle-making? The contour of a night: broken in places with sleep, evacuation, sirens, the koel's harrying keening across the tower block tops. It gets too much. You just want it to shut up. You want to fold your waking up in a cloth and bury it with the other clutter. You want traffic to stop so you can cross. You want forgetting to heal.

I had myself a very slow day. I practised age. The clock ticked past the minute I was born. I itched. I took pills. I swallowed pride: lemongrass, vanillaed eggs. I guessed the weather. Guessed wrong. Drove through rain from queue to queue. Have the privilege, at least. Of carrying the wait of the world. Everyone comes to it. Has. Will. This room with no windows. Surmised vista. One can be mindful, yes, but on what grounds vigilance? Against what? It's not so bad here: there's reading material, fresh water, bland music. Like regime change, except more like braving dentists: distraction, then extraction. What one can change: location, breath-pauses, attention. Time turns space: a fold becomes a crease. Your tracks do not say where you've been, only that the tread is worn, throat parched but whistling. The heart's haul melting in a back pocket. Because it is not night, not yet; the heat has not learnt silence. Sun's going down first: that's the plot spoilt. Sing anyway. I can tell myself from dirt.

Because the lights are the most nutritious parts, which is why predators go for the belly of a kill. The pregnant liver, the sweet enteric coil, only later the gelatinous spheres from which no fear any longer emits. Silenced, the drums. Unknotted, the taut cord of a grunt. These tunnels (irriguous, chasmal) braved and mined for precious joules. Lips do not have to be kissed to raise a colony of mitres. An old form, the oldest, of relations: be-in. What can it mean to possess anything, but to seize? As if a firm grasp might stay the sun. Which is to say: pass without comment. It has been a good ride, at least a ride. No. The fight is what's eaten. What the eating's for.

Things sensed from behind closed eyelids: A new country, nameless, loud over everything. Goods carried not in pockets but in folds of the mouth. Something very like spent stars. A circus choir travailing night's equator. Lost sleep shorn of wood, sawdusted and bleating. Lightning sieved through cheesecloth. A web-based interface with indiscrete objects. Strobe tests from a six-year-old. Figures of eight on their side. Somehow, the glut glut of drainage. Shifting gravel; cervical grot. Smudged writing: invoices, camel prices, a prescription for amnesia. A map of dead ends and the case it comes in. Every colour quiet in the pencil box. At the close of history, all that is left of the sea.

What it is like. To go blind slowly.

Even black holes let glimmers out: like the ghosts of signal, fugacious, dubitable.

They're calling a name at the nurse's station: is it yours? That's just the brain dreaming it is whole.

Sometimes the switches snap from use. Sometimes the damp gets in, or rats (ha!) chew up the circuitry and before you know it you've gone and ruined someone's retirement.

The stew a little less salty, every time. Sea stinging a little less, becoming more horizontal, more cloud.

I did not notice the edge of the glass, it was suddenly there, like bad news in the mail. Like a phone call after midnight.

A faint tea scent, like distant lips. The sun with a headcold come to collect.

Not enough to take home in a bag: finish it here, or get some help. Nobody is going to stop being happy just because you broke your eggs.

It gets night earlier and stays there.

Muffled laughter, but with photons. The pillowy underneaths of blankets. Tree bark scraped off so the sap dries out.

Did you touch me or did the feather of a crow? Speaking louder or more slowly doesn't help, you know.

Be thankful for the rest of the cutlery drawer. The stench of roses.

Get your garden ready before the gate closes.

The body registers what the mind imagines beneath notice until it becomes pressing. Reading has become a strain. The lights are either too dim to make out print on paper, or else too bright. On an iPad the text can be adjusted to suit, but the glare saps attention and focal energy from a discourse between centre and periphery. Soon there is a heaviness about the eyes, a pinching ache to the brow, a nagging intimation of violence at the margins of the face. A throbbing nod to the immanent. Shifting posture varies the light conditions, requiring a period of adjustment. Invariance in position pools acid and blood in the lower back and limbs, reducing oxygen the brain needs to follow a conceptual argument about hybrid spaces. The body is at the confluence of various insistences, one of which is read as will, another as itch. Distraction is as intimate as desire to know, as the circulatory empire of the heart, of which sentience is but a proud and prime colony. The fingers scrawl, underline, highlight, flick, scratch, tap, fondle, caress. Words on the page or on the screen: physics gesturing towards metaphysics. A billion organisms toil to keep a cognitive conurbation active so that an achievement might be unlocked, or immensity contemplated. Syllables assembled in the brain, unplayed by breath but brushed by clatter, become flicker again, boil and pulse in the eye's photonic net, strange catch on the shore of a different knowing.

> 'The hummingbirds hover in mid air desperate with agitation and blue hysteria'
> —Pooja Nansi, 'Dear Alvin'

Dear Pooja,

I want to slow down the framerate to see the chopchopchop of their pinions, their lesson that living is movement. To see what all too swiftly progresses. Too many things will soon be this grey blur as they pass me by. The heart, too, races for the cliffs, has learnt from cartoons this is how to take flight, that the fall only resets the game. All too often you hear birds before you see them, overhead, the hiphop of a hundred daily battles to mate and feed and fend. I want to know it is alright to let go of knowing. To steep, below the green canvas, in blind listening. Just as the flock of our breaths follows the long river within us home without the lead of sunlight. In the night that will soon become my day, drums roost, strings nest, words play, colourless, untethered, aloft.

If someone were to sit across from you right now, you could tell them the story of your hunger; what vacancy led you to wander beyond sight of the familiar. How it was not enough to scale the nearby hills to gaze at mountains. Foolish one, to leave the flock and its feast of grass. Sorry in the cold, sorry in the rain. And for what? The shape of stone, the contour of cliffs few have thought to measure. The heft of a pack, the feel of cheek against ungiving granite. Your weight shifting, shifting again, seeking purchase, some small niche with which to pry your way into further and further risk. Unready, but for the grip and the upward look. Madness. Bile. Blood. The stench of wet gneiss. Always, the tug backwards into the dark. The inopportune itch. If someone were to sit across from you—but that's the thing. How all you want is to sit down and be done and to tell of it. To tell that in the telling.

**Alvin Pang** is an award-winning poet and editor based in Singapore. Featured in the *Oxford Companion to Modern Poetry in English*, and the *Penguin Book of the Prose Poem*, his writing has been published in more than twenty languages. An internationally engaged literary practitioner and speaker, he is a Fellow of the Iowa International Writing Program, and a board member of the International Poetry Studies Institute. He is currently completing a PhD in creative writing practice with RMIT University. As an author and editor, he has published several volumes of poetry and anthologies of Singaporean literature. His recent books include: *When the Barbarians Arrive* (Arc Publications, UK, 2012), *UNION: 15 Years of Drunken Boat / 50 Years of Writing from Singapore* (Ethos/Drunken Boat 2015), *När barbarerna kommer* (Rámus Forlag, Sweden, 2015) and *WHAT HAPPENED: Poems 1997-2017* (Math Paper Press, 2017). Apart from finalising a volume of non-fiction vignettes, Pang is also working on a new novel exploring oceanic perspectives on desire, language, memory and confluent futures.

## IPSI: International Poetry Studies Institute

The International Poetry Studies Institute (IPSI) is part of the Centre for Creative and Cultural Research, Faculty of Arts and Design, University of Canberra. IPSI conducts research related to poetry, and publishes and promulgates the outcomes of this research internationally. The institute also publishes poetry and interviews with poets, as well as related material, from around the world. Publication of such material takes place in IPSI's online journal Axon: Creative Explorations (www.axonjournal.com.au). IPSI's goals include working – collaboratively, where possible – for the appreciation and understanding of poetry, poetic language and the cultural and social significance of poetry. The institute also organises symposia, seminars, readings and other poetry-related activities and events.

## IPSI Chapbook Series

The IPSI Chapbook Series publishes new work by leading poets from Australia and beyond. The chapbooks feature extended selections beyond the scope of most journals, highlighting innovative work by poets both new and established. The series is linked to an international program of poets in residence at the University of Canberra.
Series Editor: Paul Munden.

## CCCR: Centre for Creative & Cultural Research

The Centre for Creative and Cultural Research (CCCR) is IPSI's umbrella organisation and brings together staff, adjuncts, research students and visiting fellows who work on key challenges within the cultural sector and creative field. A central feature of its research concerns the effects of digitisation and globalisation on cultural producers, whether individuals, communities or organisations.

www.ingramcontent.com/pod-product-compliance
Ingram Content Group UK Ltd.
Pitfield, Milton Keynes, MK11 3LW, UK
UKHW021323180426
11947UKWH00017B/1411